MIND & MUSIC

TIPS AND LESSONS
from
THE GUY in the BACK ROW

BRIAN FARRELL
B.Mus.A.(Hons.), B.Ed., M.A.

www.brianfarrell.ca

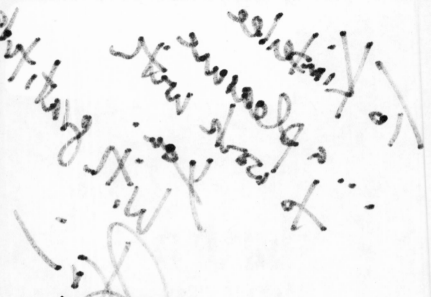

◆ FriesenPress

Suite 300 - 990 Fort St
Victoria, BC, V8V 3K2
Canada

www.friesenpress.com

ISBN
978-1-5255-3674-8 (Hardcover)
978-1-5255-3675-5 (Paperback)
978-1-5255-3676-2 (eBook)

1. MUSIC

Distributed to the trade by The Ingram Book Company

Observe, Create, Perform

To those who ever sang in front of a mirror
with a hairbrush . . . or wanted to.

TABLE OF CONTENTS

Introduction

OBSERVE
Observing People

1. Flow
2. Talk Your Walk
3. Laughter
4. Perseverance: A Story
5. Songs At Fourteen
6. Van Gogh
7. Remembering
8. Do Be Do Be Do
9. Humility: A Story
10. Character: A Story
11. Breathe
12. Groove, Story, Technique
13. The More I Know
14. Saying Yes
15. Inspiration: A Story

CREATE
Creating a Unique Voice

16. Inside The Artist's Head
17. Rehearsal Space
18. Inside The Creative: A Story
19. Right And Left
20. Imagine That

21. The Senses

22. Writing A Song

23. Your Signature Sound

24. Focus Forward

PERFORM
Performing Forward

25. Clarity Of Purpose

26. Thinking About Tomorrow

27. Creating New Habits

28. Brain Change

29. Epistemology

30. Possibility

31. Mindfulness: A Story

32. Gratitude

33. Why I Am A Teacher

About The Author

Acknowledgements

Reference List

INTRODUCTION

Brian Farrell
Vocal Coach, Music Mentor

I love listening to a great storyteller.

When I was nine, I started my life in music with lessons at the piano. At the time, I didn't realize how much my teacher would influence the way I would live my life. He was a Renaissance man—gifted, talented, and intellectual, yet also incredibly humble and generous.

His teaching helped me find my voice. As an artist and musician, he would share insights about people, music, and stories relating to life. He was never afraid to do the right thing. As a church organist, he took issue with his board of directors when they didn't allow him to play spirituals on

Sundays. Yet he had a way to get to the heart of matters and, ultimately, spirituals were played and sung at that church.

Thanks to his early influence, the joy of music surrounds my life. As a music mentor and vocal coach, I have enjoyed working with people from many walks of life—students, actors, musicians in bands, speakers, reporters, preachers, and rappers, as well as patients with Parkinson's disease, singers in choirs, singers in jazz ensembles, and singers preparing for auditions, universities, contests, tours, and recording sessions. And there are musical theatre casts, psychologists, teachers, neuroscientists, lawyers, geologists, CEOs, as well as professional and amateur athletes who inspire me in their fearlessness to step out and sing.

I enjoy a good read, especially the short to-the-point books on talent, creative thinking, humour, and music.

In this book, you'll find insights and helpful tips to inspire and develop a deeper understanding of a musical life. Watching life from the back row—close enough to see, hear, and feel the vibe, but not too close to mess up the flow—makes all the difference!

The thirty-three chapters of this book are organized into three parts: Observe, Create, and Perform. This may be the first book you read as an adult without page numbers. Feel free to observe, create, and perform your way through the book: the process that leads to excellence.

Enjoy the book. Read it in any order. Be inspired!

OBSERVE

Observing People

1. FLOW

You stumble out of bed, head to the kitchen, and open a cupboard.

What are you looking for?

A glass?

Coffee cup?

Vitamins?

Why are you even in the kitchen?

Weren't you going to call your brother?

Where's the phone? Without your glasses, you can't even see to find it!

You fumble for your eyeglasses and, after a moment, realize they're propped on your head.

When you find yourself misplacing things and anxiously searching for items in all the wrong places, that's a sign that you're not in flow. Stress, lack of sleep, hormonal changes, diet, medications, and medical conditions can contribute to brain fog.

Clear your head of the brain fog. Drink water. Breathe. Manage stress. Exercise. Eat right—your body will tell you. Find out why you are not sleeping through the night. Get your hormone balance checked.

And move.

Groove and movement inspires flow, activity, and results. When you've got flow, you are open to making the best decisions that result in positive outcomes.

Mihaly Csikszentmihalyi wrote a bestseller titled *Flow*. As a former head of the Department of Psychology at the University of Chicago, he is recognized for his study of human behaviour. Csikszentmihalyi (1990) describes flow as "the state in which people are so involved in an activity that nothing else seems to matter: the experience itself is so enjoyable that people will do it even at great cost, for the sheer sake of doing it" (p. 4).

It's a great place to be. Don't overthink. Just be in the moment. It doesn't matter who is in the room. You've done all your preparation. You've prepared all the details. All that matters now is that you're doing what you love doing.

I've shared with singers who are about to perform on big stages, "Just tell your story through your song. You'll perform hundreds of times in front of audiences. Enjoy the moment. It's a gift to share your music."

When you're in a groove, you're in rhythm—you're in flow.

2. TALK YOUR WALK

You can tell a lot about a person just by how they walk.

Watch the way a performer walks onto the stage moments before they sing their first note of music, and how a speaker walks to the podium to deliver an important speech. Watch the way a student walks into the exam room minutes before the big final exam, and notice too how a child approaches the playground and then beelines for his favourite swing after he's securely inside the park gate.

People walk with a different pace in cities like Los Angeles, Memphis, or New York.

Heat and cold affects the walking pace of the people who live there. Climate plays a big part in the way people move through their lives.

My trips to Los Angeles are focused on music: gospel churches, vocal sessions, meetings with musicians and producers. The drive through gridlocked, congested traffic certainly can affect the pace of movement. Arriving at the site, the gait can be brisk—yet the warmer temperatures of LA can relax the rhythm of my walk.

When I walk the streets of Memphis with the sun baking on the back of my neck, I mosey along. My slowed-down pace mimics the tempo of life there. At the Rendezvous Restaurant on 2nd Street, slow-cooking ribs and brisket fit with how people move in Memphis.

At B. B. King's Blues Club on Beale Street, the call-and-response of the horn section in the bands echoes the deliberate delivery of the call-and-response of Bishop Al Green and his parishioners on Sunday mornings at the Full Gospel Tabernacle Church in South Memphis. He called out, and his congregation responded.

Al Green is the noted soul singer from Memphis who charted hit after hit on the soul charts of the 1970s with songs like *"Let's Stay Together"* and *"How Do You Mend a Broken Heart?"* He started Full Gospel Tabernacle Church in Memphis with an understanding that he would not be singing the music of his chart successes in the same town as his established church.

In New York City, I run to keep up with fast-paced New Yorkers, who are intent on getting to their destinations and meeting their deadlines in what seems like record-breaking time. In Soho, Pepe Rosso, a small restaurant, serves Italian take-out to its patrons almost as fast as it's ordered. To me, rushing is burned into the psyche of New Yorkers.

Just watch—you'll know a lot about a person just by how they walk. Tempo of gait can be adjusted to assist breathing, focus, and concentration.

3. LAUGHTER

People who laugh at life experience so much more.

In my career as a teacher in the school system, I was asked to tell the "candle joke" during the teacher staff meeting at the beginning of every year. It has a long setup and short punch line, and it didn't matter how many times I told it at Crescent Heights High School; it was impossible to remain poker-faced while watching the audience's expressions as they played along with the physical movements of the joke.

I once taught a comedy course that reviewed the comedy styles of music hall through vaudeville, *The Goon Show*, *Beyond the Fringe*, *Monty Python*, *Saturday Night Live*, stand-up—all of it, laughing uproariously over comedy scripts and sketches.

Laughter is so much a part of what we do with music.

Each music class I'd begin with a joke to relax students and ready them for the lesson. As a result, the students easily remembered the material and their appreciation for music and theatre increased.

For many years, a major highlight for me was working with Parkinson's patients and their caregivers. Initially, I was asked by a facilitator at Parkinson Alberta to explain the anatomy and physiology of the human voice to the group.

"Why?" I asked. "I'd be more interested in activities that would enhance their voices in a community where they'd sing together regularly." It's more important to share the various experiences of what I've learned in over 35,000 hours with singers.

That's what we did and what we continue to do. We've been singing for years now, and as I did with my high school students, I begin class with a joke. I'll play a few notes and ask, "What's this song?" After three notes, some eager participants yell out, "*Three Blind Mice!*"

And even though it's the same tune as "*Three Blind Mice,*" I say, "Noo . . . no! It's the theme song to *The Three Stooges!*" It's become a regular joke. I play the same three notes and ask, "What's this song?" And each time they shout, "*Three Blind Mice!*" You know the rest.

Laughing boosts endorphins in the brain. We remember easier. Our cheerful disposition influences others in the room. Laughter invites others to participate wholeheartedly in the singing activity. Voices are activated. Bodies are engaged!

Share a hilarious story that resonates with your audience and everyone in the room is beaming. When was the last time you laughed hysterically?

Laughter, like singing, is great brain fitness.

Laugh—you'll be inspired!

4. PERSEVERANCE: A STORY

Music And Comedy

Dudley Moore was a major influence out of England on the comedy of his day. His style of humour with Peter Cook in the revue *Beyond the Fringe*, was an inspiration for *Monty Python* in Britain, and for *Saturday Night Live* in America.

He was also an exceptional jazz composer and pianist, as well as an actor who starred in the hit movie, *10*, with Bo Derek and in the title role of the blockbuster film, *Arthur*.

These performances embody farce, satire, parody, improv, stand-up, the pregnant pause, and beats: Comedy 101.

In the mid '90s, I was teaching musical theatre at Sir Winston Churchill High School in Calgary, and in late spring, the students were scheduled to perform a full week's run of *The Mystery of Edwin Drood*, a musical peppered with music hall British comedy—a little like American vaudeville, but rooted in British farce, satire, and parody.

The comedy in *Edwin Drood* required more than a basic understanding of comedy for the show to be a success, especially for a high school audience with a serious appreciation of musical theatre and drama.

To learn more about British comedy, I researched another show that lived in the *Beyond the Fringe* model of absolute farce. It was a radio program called *The Goon Show* with Peter Sellers, Spike Milligan, and Harry Secombe. I listened to episode after episode of their hilarity until I got the rhythm of British comedy.

If there were anyone in the world who could bring an understanding of British comedy to our high school student cast of *Edwin Drood*, it would be Dudley Moore.

The Contact

The story begins here.

In the spring of 1996, Dudley Moore was scheduled to perform in Calgary with the Philharmonic to a sold-out crowd at the Southern Jubilee Auditorium just weeks before our run of *Edwin Drood*.

Weeks earlier, I'd met the manager of the Calgary Philharmonic when the musical theatre student actors and dancers had performed with the Philharmonic, and he'd given me the contact information for Moore's agent in New York. The next day, I called and Moore's agent said he'd contact his client and get back to me.

Then, I told the cast of *Edwin Drood* we had a chance to meet and talk with Dudley Moore, and, I added, it would likely be a last-minute arrangement. To be ready, I asked them to take the permission forms home and have their parents sign and return them to me by the next day.

Now, it was a week before Moore's concert in Calgary. From our end, we had everything covered: booking a school bus and driver, as well as informing parents, the school principal, and teachers.

We waited.

Long Line In

On Friday morning, I was chairing the Fine Arts Department meeting when Moore's agent called to say Dudley Moore would meet the students later that morning after his rehearsal with the Philharmonic.

Using the school's public address system, I let the cast of *Edwin Drood* know we'd be meeting in the lobby immediately, and I'd collect the approval forms their parents had signed.

There was a teacher to cover my morning classes, and the banana bus was fired up and ready to go. Greg, the head of the Phys. Ed Department, was our driver. We had just thirty minutes to get to the Southern Jubilee Auditorium before the rehearsal startup.

We arrived at our destination minutes before the rehearsal start time. Student cast members poured out of the bus and gathered at the backstage door entrance as I explained the reason for our visit to the stage door security guard.

But he said, "You can't enter the rehearsal hall. It's closed to the public."

Fortunately, the manager of the Philharmonic had arrived, and I caught his attention.

"Brian, what are you doing here?" he asked.

Hearing me out, he answered, "I don't think Dudley Moore even knows you're here with all these students."

"It would be great if you could just get us inside the rehearsal," I said.

And with that, he kindly arranged with the stage door security guard to let us in.

We walked through the back hallway of the auditorium to a side door and entered the orchestra seating area. We sat down about ten rows from center stage as the orchestra was about to begin.

Dudley Moore sat at the Steinway concert grand piano. The orchestra players were in position. Conductor Victor Sawa was ready to wield his baton to cue the first note when, instead, he turned from the orchestra and faced us. We were easy to spot in a closed public rehearsal hall.

"Brian, come on up here. I want you to meet Mr. Dudley Moore," he said.

I climbed onto the stage, shook hands, and whispered to Mr. Moore, "Did you know we were coming here to talk with you about *Edwin Drood*?"

With his distinct English accent, he said, "Didn't know that, but how about after the Mozart, during the break, I'll talk with the students?"

It was a day to remember.

A New Level of Excellence

Meeting Dudley Moore was a great experience. We appreciated him as a pianist, a comedian, and as a generous human being. He took his time while answering our questions about British comedy, and he inspired the cast to reach a new level of excellence during our weeklong, sold-out production of *Edwin Drood*. Every night the students impressed their audience and me.

Years later, Raghav, a member of that same high school cast of *Edwin Drood*, became an international success as a singer with hit after hit song on the British charts. He travelled extensively, and on one of his many trips to New York, he saw the musical, *Edwin Drood*, on the Broadway stage and called me after, saying, "Our high school cast got it! We really were that good!"

In 2016, when I was in New York, I met Bo Derek and John Corbett by chance at the Cafe Luxembourg on the Upper West Side sitting at the table on my right, celebrating the release of Corbett's film *My Big Fat Greek Wedding 2*.

I introduced myself after dinner, and I shared how great it had been for my high school actors and me to meet Dudley Moore. I knew Bo's debut with him in the movie *10* was significant for her. At the box office, the Hollywood smash movie made Bo Derek and Dudley Moore acclaimed superstars in America.

She turned to her partner, John Corbett. "Dudley was such a wonderful man—he was so kind to me when we worked together."

Perseverance always pays off. It will move you forward toward what you really want.

5. SONGS AT FOURTEEN

When I search for songs to share with the Parkinson's singers, I select numbers that are fun to sing, relatable, and represent stories inside their lives. We sing together for a ninety-minute class on Wednesday mornings.

It has to be the right style and rhythm of music for each patient. When the Parkinson's singers walk around the room to the rhythm of the music, they walk with energy and confidence. They walk to the tempo of the song. There is a connection to self and a connection to others in the room. Individuals are upbeat and joyful as they move around the room to the music.

On the internet, there's an example of a man with Parkinson's disease using his walker haltingly as he navigates his kitchen, but as soon as he puts a headset on to listen to music with a strong rhythmic element, his gait changes from tentative, teetering steps to confident, consistent strides.

The tunes we enjoy singing include songs like *"For Me and My Gal"* (1917), *"Blue Skies"* (1926), and *"Happy Days are Here Again"* (1929), the latter of which, not surprisingly, was written at the onset of the Great Depression in October 1929. Then there's *"You're Nobody till Somebody Loves You"* (1944), *"A White Sport Coat"* (1957), *"Downtown"* (1964), and *"Everybody Loves Somebody Sometime"* (1964).

Many of these songs were popular when the Parkinson's patients were around fourteen years old. Life was taking shape. They had one foot in childhood and the other in youth. They were changing—physically, mentally, emotionally, and musically.

In a recent *New York Times* article titled "The Songs That Bind," Seth Stephens-Davidowitz (2018) writes, "The most important period for men in forming their adult tastes were the ages 13–16. What about women? On average, their favourite songs came out when they were 13. The most important period for women is the ages 11–14" *(p. 9)*.

What can that mean if you were born in 1954? You would have been fourteen years old when "Tiptoe Through the Tulips" was re-released in 1968 by a quirky, quivery, falsetto-voiced ukulele player named Tiny Tim. And it played and played and replayed on television talk shows.

My grandfather believed Tiny Tim did a good job with that old tune, originally written in 1929, but my father thought otherwise. I think the very appearance of Tiny Tim was enough for him. Growing up in our home,

I often looked at my dad's framed photo in his neatly pressed American Navy uniform that was in sharp contrast to Tiny Tim's vaudeville consignment garb.

William Grimes (1996) in a *New York Times* article described Tiny Tim as "a pear-shaped singer with a beak nose, scraggly shoulder-length hair and an outfit that could be described as haute-couture bum." I think my dad listened to Tiny Tim with William's eyes.

As for me, I wasn't all that interested—I was born after 1954.

The songs that hit the charts during my fourteenth year were *"American Woman"* by the Guess Who and *"Close to You"* by the Carpenters.

The Guess Who album, *American Woman*, was their biggest album by far and stayed on the charts for over a year. The Carpenters album, *Close to You*, is still rated in the top 500 greatest albums of all time by *Rolling Stone* magazine.

Think back: What is the soundtrack of your childhood memories?

6. VAN GOGH

When Lori Lieberman heard singer/songwriter Don McLean's performance of *"Empty Chairs"* at the Troubadour Club in Los Angeles, she felt like he was singing it directly to her. McLean was heavily influenced by Vincent van Gogh's painting *Vincent's Chair with His Pipe,* which called up the angst and pain inside the mind of the artist.

"Killing Me Softly" was then written in collaboration with Lori Lieberman, Charles Fox, and Norman Gimbel and recorded in late 1971 by Lieberman. Roberta Flack said the song "found her" when she heard Lieberman's performance of the song on an airline playlist and passionately released her version in 1973 winning the 1973 Grammy Award for Record of the Year, Best Pop Vocal Performance Female, and Song of the Year. In 1997, sung by the Fugees with Lauren Hill, it again won a Grammy for Best R & B Performance by a Duo or Group with Vocal.

The song *"Vincent"* by Don McLean recalls a similar artistic experience to *"Killing Me Softly"* in that the genesis of that song came to him after reading a Van Gogh biography. With a print of Van Gogh's painting *Starry Night* before him, McLean wrote the words on a paper bag and his masterpiece song begins with the infamous line "Starry, starry night."

At my studio on a cloudy morning, with the lights turned up full, Norm, an intuitive singer, pointed to the lid of the ebony polished grand piano and exclaimed, "Van Gogh!"

And sure enough, with the pot lights beaming down on the shining surface, whiteness swirled like Van Gogh's brushstrokes in his timeless masterpiece, *Starry Night*.

Enduring songs are rich in emotion and metaphor.

7. REMEMBERING

It's amazing to me how singers remember words and melodies.

In the world of music, there are individuals who can hear a symphony once then play it on a piano. Russian composer, pianist, and conductor Sergei Rachmaninoff could do just that. He could recall lengthy melodies heard even years before. That's a gift.

In the book *Leadership Jazz*, Max DePree (1992) notes that everyone in a jazz band plays together, and at times, performs certain sections as soloists. Even so, the players in the jazz band have total regard for the overall blend and balance of the sound.

Calgary Choral Society was established in 1952 for Queen Elizabeth's coronation and performed musical works for choir with orchestra and soloists.

When I took on the responsibilities of Artistic Director in 1995, I asked the group to sing off-book. With the musical parts memorized and unimpeded by print music, the group can focus on blend, balance, vocal colour, dynamics, story, style, choreographed movement, and so much more.

Each singer memorizes about twenty-two songs written in four to eight parts for a concert. Styles range from gospel, spirituals, R & B, soul, Motown, pop, rock, contemporary, and rap. Choral and band arrangements from five decades of music are customized to represent the signature sound of the group.

In 2008, we re-branded as Revv52: "Revv," as in revolution and expanding the boundaries of choral music, and "52," representing the year the group was founded.

Revv52 is a group of fifty-five auditioned singers and six band members. The performances are riveting both technically and visually, expressing the story inside each song.

The singers learn the words and music quickly. My head tilts like a terrier's when a singer mouths the wrong words to a song. It's like watching someone speak a made-up language for a bad movie dub. To help singers at Revv52, we orientate each singer with a number of learning tools to help through the process: their individual parts are recorded for them; we record the entire show for review weeks before the performance; various sectional rehearsals happen outside the weekly group rehearsal; and full-day workshops with the band and the singers help establish the overall flow of the show.

At Revv52, singers have had to learn how to memorize their parts. Everyone has their own way of remembering. Some singers have the ability to remember lyrics more than the music. Others learn music quicker than the lyrics. There are also non-music readers with an uncanny ability to remember both words and music.

A surprising number of brilliant musicians don't read music but have the ability to bring a song to life in performance. Michael Jackson could do it. And so could Frank Sinatra.

Remembering the content, the words, the music, and the technique lead to freedom of expression and mastery. You become a better storyteller and the group works as one.

8. DO BE DO BE DO

Each year I audition singing candidates for the performance group Revv52: that's the fifty-five voice ensemble with a band that sings a variety of musical styles from five decades of music.

The vision of Revv52 is "To be recognized as a leader in Canada's vocal and performing arts communities, fusing a variety of creative elements to produce performances that entertain and open the hearts and minds of audiences everywhere."

Singers are nervous during the audition, and I want to make it a really positive experience for them. I ask for these five things:

1. Sing a song of your choosing in whatever style you wish.

2. Sing pitches played on a piano in your vocal range as well as outside of your vocal range.

3. Sing a short sight passage taken from a Revv52 arranged vocal score.

4. Clap a short rhythmic passage that includes a variety of note values and rests.

5. Scat sing a twelve-bar blues passage. Scat singing is vocal improvisation where the singer improvises on melody and rhythm using their voice as an instrument.

For me, the scat portion of the audition tells me a lot about the singer. It tells me how fearless they are to improvise. It tells me how they listen to groove and tempo and how they create space inside the musical line. It tells me a lot about the styles of music they are familiar with and where they are comfortable. And it tells me how they think. Do they think in layers by adding melodic riffs inside their scat improvisation?

Listen to Ella Fitzgerald sing *"Airmail Special."* Most horn players assimilate the sound of singers in their performances. Ella listened to great horn players to craft her style as one of the finest American scat singers.

Scat singing is the secret sauce of groove with style. It reveals so much about the singer and their personal story.

Do. Be.

9. HUMILITY: A STORY

Background

Paul Brandt is the most awarded male country artist in the history of Canadian music.

As part of a Canada-wide celebration of music education, Paul wrote a letter to a music teacher who influenced his dream. It gives a brief backstory on his beginnings in music. I was honoured to receive this:

> *Twenty-three years ago at Crescent Heights High School, there was a self-conscious, painfully shy young man who enjoyed basketball, and secretly writing music, playing guitar, and singing. That young man was me.*
>
> *Your passion for music and your dedication to excellence in the classroom was*

what sold me. It was obvious to everyone in the class that you actually cared about teaching, and about being great in music. It was also clear you cared about us.

Until you took notice, it never occurred to me that anybody other than my parents would ever think I was much good at anything at all, let alone music. And I never would have thought that I'd be living the music dream I'm living today. You are the real deal. (P. Brandt, personal communication, May 1, 2013)

It wasn't till his last year in high school that Paul decided to try on some music classes. As he mentioned in the letter, he enjoyed basketball.

I recall significant experiences during his final year of high school that turned attention to his musical talent. Paul wrote exceptional songs in music class. And when he sang, people listened. There was his first big solo on Remembrance Day in front of the entire school body, a remarkable solo in a mass high school choir performance, and his *"Amazing Grace"* solo at the Jubilee Auditorium for graduation. Each time his confidence grew and more people witnessed that unique lyric baritone voice.

The Music

After his graduation from Crescent Heights High School, Paul studied nursing at Mount Royal College in Calgary. I would invite him to stop by Sir Winston Churchill High

School where I was teaching to sing his songs for the students. He would arrive wearing that signature black cowboy hat. His songs were riveting. Paul Brandt had a gift.

Not long after the days of playing for students in a classroom, there was the night at Calgary's Longhorn Saloon. I sat with Paul's family watching the entire event from a balcony.

Paige Levy, VP of Artists & Repertoire at Warner/ Reprise Nashville, flew up from Nashville to listen to Paul perform his prepared set of songs before a live audience. It was rare for a Nashville record label exec to travel outside America to hear an artist.

And it was rare for a young Canadian singer/ songwriter to be signed to an initial deal with Warner Brothers Nashville. It all happened for Paul Brandt after that performance.

Paul is a Christian. He lives his life based on his deep faith. I once shared with Paul that his Christian example might be best realized through his actions as an artist, and not by releasing Christian songs. That changed for me in 2012.

I heard Paul's country/bluegrass collection of his favourite hymns titled *Just as I Am*. It was recorded "off the floor" at the Ryman Auditorium in Nashville with some of Nashville's finest players. For me, this is one of Paul's greatest achievements. The hymns "sing story," and the performances are exceptional. Guest vocalists and instrumentalists include Patty Loveless, John Anderson,

Ricky Skaggs, The Whites, The Isaacs, High Valley, and producer/pianist Gordon Mote.

This is an example of humility—everyone in the band gives musical space to one another; it's a lesson on how to play as a band in a band. Everyone on stage shines. This is a great example to church musicians on how to work together and how to focus on "story" inside each song.

Paul's performances of *"Amazing Grace"* provide an example of humility. His performance of that classic on the historic Ryman stage comes full circle from his high school graduation solo. That is one of the greatest songs of hope ever written.

Ironically, humility is conveyed without even knowing it.

10. CHARACTER:
A STORY

Drama

"I had him by the ankle! I had him by the ankle!"

That's what I heard as the female dancer raced from the change room and into the musical theatre classroom.

As a teacher, I worked regularly alongside three outstanding professional female choreographers. It was a real privilege to work with these women in schools: Michelle Walton at Crescent Heights High School and Sir Winston Churchill High School; Margot McDermott and Kyrsten Blair at Master's Academy and College. There was a genuine respect among students for their talents and their approach.

Back to the story . . . The dancer heard sounds and noticed movement above the ceiling tiles in the change room where female dancers changed into their dance-wear. She spotted a male student peering through the ceiling panels above the change area. As the male student scrambled to escape back through the ceiling passage, his leg broke through one of the flimsy white panels. The female dancer fumbled to grab his ankle. He escaped and was up and gone.

Immediately, the word was out!

With the news now blitzing through the school by word of mouth, it didn't take long to find the guilty party. The student network can sometimes serve up fast justice.

The person "in the ceiling" turned out to be the quarterback of the high school football team.

Resolved

The school principal and I met within minutes of the occurrence. We mutually decided that the principal would meet with the boy and his parents, and we would gather all the female musical theatre students together. The guilty offender would apologize to each of the girls, one by one, face to face. I would be there to support the girls and witness the apologies.

It ultimately worked out. The boy's parents supported the process. He was suspended from school for a few days, and his playing season as a high school quarterback was cut short. The female dancers accepted the student's sincerest apologies.

Recognizing the importance of the #MeToo international movement against sexual harassment and assault, it's heartening to know that we dealt with this matter immediately and openly. Everyone moved on.

It's good for all of us to forgive, move on, and learn from our mistakes. Life is too short to hold on to the past.

11. BREATHE

Breathe.

Some say this is at the heart of it all—a way to access the deepest regions of one's mind.

Breathe.

Being grounded and anchored from the floor on up through your legs, to your thighs, into your belly, upper chest, open throat, and into your facial mask. It's all rooted in breathing and being grounded in your body—a major principle of yoga and meditation.

Breathe.

It's not much different in sports.

Former NHL hockey star, Theo Fleury, who is also a very good singer, reminded me of this. He's grounded and anchored in his five-foot six-inch frame. It was very difficult to move Theo off the puck during his playing days. He was able to relate all of this to his singing and to his breathing. He was firmly grounded when he belted out his country favourites in my home studio as he prepped for performances.

Breathe.

I listened to Wim Hof speak about breathing. He's the guy who established records for swimming underwater in frigid temperatures at Antarctica for lengthy periods without oxygen support. Under extreme frigid conditions that would cause cardiac arrest to most people, Hof is able to sustain a normal body temperature and avoid hypothermia. It all stems from his breathing.

Breathe.

Breathing sustains calm—it helps focus. Taking a low breath allows the singer to sing through the long phrase of a musical line. The song's story then takes on meaning. When a singer breathes with low, connected breaths, the listener responds and aligns with their story.

Breathe.

The story is believable.

You become one with your soul.

12. GROOVE, STORY, TECHNIQUE

In my experience, technique is much easier to develop when the singer focuses on groove and then on story.

In many traditional conservatory music schools, technique is applied first—even before a song is placed in front of the singer. Victor Wooten, a Grammy Award-winning bassist, in his book, *The Music Lesson*, reaffirms the importance of establishing groove first. Technique is much easier to facilitate with a strong sense of groove, according to Wooten.

To acquaint the singer with style and technique at a vocal session, I sing the opening line of Elton John's "*Your Song.*" To prove a point, I sing it like Will Ferrell in a *Saturday Night Live* skit. Singing that song with a rounded "ah" vowel sound is totally out of style. Singing pop, rhythm and blues, rock, country, folk, or more contemporary music requires more attention to the consonant.

Sinatra was the master of this style of singing on the consonant. Sinatra would warm the words inside his musical phases by elongating or exaggerating the consonant. He lengthens the word "warm-m-m" in the song "*Let it Snow*" and accentuates the word "c-cold" in "*The Way You Look Tonight.*"

On the other hand, singing Handel's *Messiah* (written in 1741) with deliberate articulation on consonants leaves little room for Handel's beautiful sonorous melodies to come alive. For baroque, classical, or romantic styles, singing with focus on vowels is most appropriate.

Stylizing a song is so much part of the believability factor for a listener. The song has to draw the listener in. Groove and story will help make aspects of technique easier for the singer.

Groove, story, and technique connect to a rhythm of life.

13. THE MORE I KNOW

After watching shows like *American Idol*, *The Voice*, or *America's Got Talent*, it seems that everyone has become an expert.

We think we know. We've learned a little along the way about singing through the feedback from judges or the inside stories shared about participants. We now believe we know.

There's a poem I enjoy reading that was written by Ronald David Laing. As a Scottish psychiatrist and writer, R. D. Laing wrote almost exclusively on mental illness and notably the experience of psychosis. The poem is titled "*There is Something I Don't Know*" (1972).

It revolves around the anxiety of not knowing something. The poet believes he should know what it is he doesn't know; however, because he doesn't want to look "stupid," he pretends to know it. This assumption leads to many other assumptions about pretending to know "everything" . . . and pretending to know everything is such a limiting assumption. Exhausting.

I find the more I know, the more I don't know. I start to realize there are more and more galaxies out there to discover just when I get comfortable with my own little neighbourhood one. With that in mind, I continue to try on new ideas.

When someone rambles on and on, pretending to know everything, this poem comes to mind. Not good.

Listening is good. And so are the inimitable relationships that result.

14. SAYING YES

As our son and daughter grew older, they challenged the thinking and planning of my wife and I as we tried to keep the doors of future possibility open for them.

As Ryan was about to enter his grade 11 year of high school, he asked to attend hockey school and play in Saskatchewan, which was an eight-hour drive from where we live. Days before, he was the last cut from a Calgary AA hockey team and forced to play at a high community level. He was determined to keep his options open so that he could play college hockey in the United States. To do so, he would have to play in a league higher than community level to qualify for consideration at an American college.

Ryan was a hockey player who also played the violin well enough to qualify for a performance degree. But he stayed committed to making something happen with hockey.

We said yes to Saskatchewan, yes to the minus 50 degrees Celsius Saskatchewan winter, and yes to a year away from Calgary during an important academic year.

The hockey school in Saskatchewan kept Ryan's dream alive. He ultimately received a scholarship as an academic, hockey-playing violinist to Trinity College in Hartford, Connecticut, then continued his pursuits to Ohio State and Rush University Medical School in Chicago. His urologic surgery residency drew on his attention to detail and precision as a violinist and his collaborative hockey team mindset. These characteristics opened doors for him to work with a "hall of fame" surgeon and mentor. The best professionals want to work with those who dare to say "yes."

Our daughter, Lauren, was passionate about singing, dancing, and acting after high school leading her to audition at noted performing arts universities. We said yes to a gruelling audition preparation and trek through Syracuse, Boston, Ann Arbor, Cincinnati, Pittsburgh, Tucson, and Edmonton.

The audition journey led her to the University of Arizona in Tucson where she graduated with a BFA in theatre and dance. She's currently a respected freelance producer and director in New York City working with notable, award-winning actors, creatives, and crew who have huge trust in her ability to create, collaborate, and budget for world-class clients.

In retrospect, setting the bar high worked out well for both Ryan and Lauren. They set their sights on schools that would fuel their ambitions and their futures.

We didn't say no to our kids—we reinforced, supported, and opened doors to possibilities.

The path is not always linear, and it requires flexible thinking. Rule #6, as shared by world-renowned conductor Benjamin Zander and psychotherapist Rosamund Stone Zander (2000) in *The Art of Possibility*, is this: "Don't take yourself so g-damn seriously" (p. 78).

Think big! Go for it!

15. INSPIRATION: A STORY

Inspire Higher

Alvin Law was a drummer, a skier, a keyboard player, trombonist, and in demand as an exceptional motivational speaker. He lived in Yorkton, Saskatchewan.

His mother had used the drug thalidomide while pregnant, which resulted in his congenital disorder. Alvin Law was born without arms. He was a child of thalidomide.

I wanted him to come to Calgary to address an assembly of students at Crescent Heights High School.

I called Alvin at his home and asked whether he'd be interested in speaking at the school. He said to make the trip worthwhile, he would have to speak at about five Calgary area schools. I said I could arrange that.

After calling around to organize Alvin's high school visits, I met with him at a local restaurant to review details.

Walking into the restaurant, I recognized him sitting with a group of people at a nearby table. As I approached the group, I was surprised to see he was eating chicken wings. Watching Alvin eating chicken wings with his feet was a trip.

As I grew to know him over the course of his short time in Calgary, the chicken wing experience was of little consequence. He was extraordinary in so many significant ways.

For the trip to the five Calgary schools, I arranged a rented vehicle for him. No chaperone was necessary—he drove. Watching Alvin Law approach the car, unlock the door manually with his foot, plant himself into the driver's seat, adjust his seat for comfort, and then drive away blew my mind.

He said it was always fun for him to watch the stare from other drivers at stoplights. He liked to wave with his foot to drivers at stops. Then with his foot on the wheel and the other on the gas, he'd move on.

A Mic, a Piano, and a Drum

He asked that I provide a mic, a piano keyboard, and a snare drum to be placed onstage for each of his school visits. He would play the instruments one at a time in a mini-recital. He was very musical.

In front of student audiences, Alvin was magic. He'd walk the stage and transfix audiences with his stories of persevering and overcoming obstacles.

He told me a story about Billy Joel. I know a little about the singer. My wife grew up in Harrow, a small town in Ontario. Her neighbour, Bob Thrasher, was a diesel

mechanic there who became road manager and then production manager for Billy Joel. Thanks to Bob, we've seen
a few concerts up close.

Alvin shared *his* Billy Joel experience. Billy's drummer
at the time was Liberty DeVito. During a sound check in
Edmonton, Liberty thought it would be hilarious to ask
Alvin, who attended the sound check, to sit at the drum
set and play along without telling Billy.

Alvin sat in and played during a portion of the sound
check. Billy Joel went ballistic!

While Alvin is a fine drummer, a guy playing drums
with no arms doesn't sound like Liberty DeVito.

After the sound check, he was introduced to Billy;
according to Alvin, it was a good meeting.

In the song *"We Didn't Start the Fire,"* there is a reference to "children of thalidomide."

Alvin takes credit for that.

Whenever I hear that Billy Joel song, I think of Alvin.

CREATE

Creating a Unique Voice

16. INSIDE THE ARTIST'S HEAD

You're often closest to a breakthrough when you're furthest away. Bob Dylan talked about that before he wrote his masterpiece, *"Like a Rolling Stone."* He was ready to give up.

Outside the artist's head, there can be the swagger and attitude of a Sinatra—inside their head can be a cacophony of noise.

Artists think about their "why." They go inside and back. Something summons them to music, to art. It nurtures, soothes, and stirs them. Noise disturbs the inner solace of where an artist lives creatively.

They go "inside" to create. It can be a lonely place, but it's where they want to be—away from the noise, the didactic ranting of the masses about how to create.

It can be very simple. It's in the easiness and carefreeness of a child where the creative lives. It's not easy for all artists. Some are wrapped in a melancholy that underlies a darker side. Some are inspired by the fear of failing or a relentless pursuit to be better. Sometimes their creative genius isn't fully realized till years later.

But in the childlike ease of the creative, the noise stops and the fear is gone, the self-doubt and loathing fall away. Trust and the bigger universe opens up. Some call it the ghost or the divine, but it is there for the artist when they "release."

The artistic mind never registers on a scale of normal. It challenges the status quo and rallies against rules and establishment expectations.

Artists go to their art for strength and purpose. They listen, feel, see, taste, and remember.

Artists know when they are in that state of *flow* and when they aren't. They know when they are enlightened by a muse, the divine, or the ghost, and they get out of their own way to create again.

How do you create?

17. REHEARSAL SPACE

It's wonderful to work with singers in a creative space where learning is fun.

In the music studio, I open the blinds to a backyard acreage frequented by deer, coyotes, squirrels, jackrabbits, hawks, owls, the occasional moose, our Welsh Terrier, Gadsby, and our Australian Shepherd, Duke. On clear, brisk winter days, the view of the Rocky Mountains is awe-inspiring.

Singers have choices among what microphones to use. To accompany singers, I access digital keyboards or a grand piano. Guitars and percussion instruments are displayed, ready to play. An LCD screen is central in the room where singers can view video examples of performances or song charts. For feedback, it's helpful to record and play back a section of their singing. Technology is at our fingertips. A large mirror allows them to check their overall posture and breathing technique. An adjoining library is filled with books and music readily accessible for the singer.

For me, this environment encourages creativity. For singers, it's exciting to have access to the musical instruments and equipment as well as the inspiring view.

I conduct workshops at The Annex in Calgary, a space built by my good friend, Dan, as a tribute to his late wife, Michelle. It's a spectacular venue for workshop participants. The Annex is built in the style of a Chicago or New York speakeasy with big screen, surround-sound speakers, a large performance stage for soloists and bands, comfortable leather chairs, and cushy couches. A long, Chicago-bricked bar stocked with an arsenal of libations lines the west wall. It's "vibey" and a great space to create.

An ideal space is one where the artist can think alone and work collaboratively when necessary. My home studio and The Annex provide opportunity for exceptional creative experiences.

A supportive and safe space opens the door to more inspired creativity.

Do you have a space that inspires your creativity?

18. INSIDE THE CREATIVE: A STORY

The Village

I love New York: the food, Broadway, Jazz at Lincoln Center, the clubs, the little bookstore at Julliard, Central Park, the High Line, Yankees and Mets baseball, the Chelsea Market.

I visit New York at least twice a year. Our daughter is a producer/director there. Every time I visit, I take the subway to Greenwich Village and walk the streets. I visit Jamal, the owner at Village Music World on Bleecker Street, and Bob at House of Oldies on Carmine Street. Then I cross the street to say hello to Jim at Unoppressive Non-Imperialist Bargain Books and browse their eclectic and unique selections of literature.

A couple of doors down is Carmine Street Guitars, known for building custom handmade guitars from the reconstructed wood of gutted buildings in the Bowery neighbourhood. Rick Kelly, owner and guitar maker, refers to the wood as the "bones of New York City." Rick is usually in and always friendly.

Around the corner from Carmine Street is Pasticceria Rocco on Bleecker Street. The cannoli in this place is worth the stop. I rarely eat dessert, but in New York, I make a point to eat it here. I sit at a little table at the front of the restaurant, near the multi-coloured display case of Italian baked goods, and order a cannoli and espresso with cream.

For me, that's a New York experience!

The Boulevardier

I know my way around the Village better these days. The streets can wind confusingly.

I once spent a half-day in this neighbourhood looking for the Waverly Inn, passing it twice without even knowing.

I wanted to see the Edward Sorel mural in the restaurant. *The New York Times* hails him as one of America's foremost political satirists. His work has appeared in *Vanity Fair*, *The Nation*, *The Atlantic*, and *New York Magazine*.

When I finally arrived at the Waverly Inn, I stepped inside and asked, "Could I look inside the restaurant and snap a picture of the mural?"

"No pictures allowed, sir."

So I sat at the corner of the bar just outside the entrance to the restaurant. It was mid-afternoon, and local patrons started to crowd around the bar. I ordered a drink from the menu.

After I received my cocktail, I asked the bartender about the mural and how he liked his work at the Waverly. I received not much more than a nod and a short grunt. He wasn't too conversational—until I said, "I'm not big on this first cocktail. Could you make me a boulevardier?" And suddenly he came alive.

"It's my wife's favourite cocktail," he said. He proceeded to mix one for me: ice, sweet vermouth, Campari, bourbon, and a twist of lemon.

It was splendid. I asked about the bourbon in the cocktail.

"Medley Brothers."

After the last sip of my boulevardier, I paid my tab and thanked him.

"Try this . . . on me." He handed me a glass of one of their top-shelf bourbons to sample.

I did manage to get a photo of the Edward Sorel mural inside the restaurant. Painted on the two-panel mural that covered the walls, I recognized the caricatures of Walt Whitman, Truman Capote, Dylan Thomas, Jack Kerouac, Norman Mailer, Jackson Pollack, James Baldwin, Thelonius Monk, Bob Dylan, Joan Baez, Andy Warhol, Fran Lebowitz, and Marlon Brando. There were more famous faces of those who once frequented the Waverly, but I didn't want to overstay my welcome. I made a quick exit.

I left the Waverly Inn at 16 Bank Street after two cocktails, a special top-shelf bourbon, and a new zeal for navigating my way through the Village.

The Chelsea Hotel

The first time I stayed in the Village was a ten-day span of time. I was doing research on the Village music scene for a series of Calgary shows I would be conducting. I walked in circles trying to get my bearings. These streets haven't changed much since the late 1700s.

During the summer of 2010, I stayed at the twelve-story Chelsea Hotel at 222 West 23rd Street.

Noted literary and visual artists, actors, directors, musicians, and fashion designers resided at the Chelsea like Janis Joplin. Listen to Leonard Cohen's "Chelsea Hotel #2" to know more about Janis. Arthur C. Clarke wrote *A Space Odyssey* here. Dylan Thomas drank more than a few here. Sid Vicious was charged with stabbing and killing his girlfriend, Nancy Spungen, in Room 100. Arthur Miller found the hotel a place of quietude after Marilyn Monroe's death. There were many more distinct individuals who called the Chelsea home. Tom Wolfe, Mark Twain, Christopher Beane, Willem de Kooning, Bob Dylan, Sean Lennon, the Mamas and the Papas, the Grateful Dead all stayed at "the hotel that art calls home"—which is what the writer Michael T. Kaufman referred to the hotel as in the October 14, 1994 edition of *The New York Times*.

Jerry Weinstein was a mainstay at the hotel, hired back in the late '70s by his friend and then manager, Stanley Bard. He knew the full-blown history of the Chelsea and conducted tours of the suites and rooms of artists who had resided there.

Each day when I returned to the hotel, I'd meet Jerry at the front desk behind the lobby.

The Village Voice

The Chelsea closed its doors to guests in August 2011 for its current renovation that is expected to continue through 2019. Its rich history could be seen everywhere. The art hung on the walls of each floor represented the work of artists who once lived or currently reside at the Chelsea. Instead of paying rent, their art was a way of securing their stay.

I once met with a particular (and peculiar) musician in the lobby.

After my first day wandering through the Village, I returned to the hotel lobby and noticed a group of four men huddled around a small table. They carried on in animated discussion, and I learned they met every afternoon at that table.

I asked Jerry, the front desk manager, whom I could contact in that group to learn more about the music scene in the Village. He told me that one of the artists played in a renowned New York surfer band called the Surftones.

His name was Tim Sullivan, and he'd been living at the Chelsea since the '80s. Whenever I saw Tim in the lobby, he wore long shorts to his knees with a T-shirt and nondescript baseball cap.

When Jerry handed me Tim's contact number at the hotel, I called and immediately made an appointment to meet with him the next afternoon.

The lobby was rich with unique, multi-coloured paintings, and hanging from the ceiling was a sculpture of a little girl on a swing. During our meeting under the girl on a swing, Tim filled me in on the Village—what to see and who to see. It was an extraordinary encounter. He had an encyclopedic knowledge of the hotel and the Village music scene.

He talked about artists of the '60s in the Village: Dylan, Dave Van Ronk, the Velvet Underground, the Clancy Brothers, Joan Baez, Phil Ochs, Richie Havens, Tom Paxton, and so many more. It was a heated decade that included the Stonewall Riots by the LGBT community against a police raid at the Stonewall Inn and civil rights rallies at Washington Square Park.

The artists in the Village during these times were dangerous, and they were unafraid.

At the Bitter End

One of the places Tim referred me to was The Bitter End, a legendary New York rock 'n' roll nightclub established in 1960. Every major folk, pop, and rock artist of the '60s and '70s played there. It's a haven for a variety of artists: Stevie Wonder, Bob Dylan, Lady Gaga, Jackson Browne, Neil Diamond, Gavin DeGraw, Woody Allen, Jon Stewart, Randy Newman, Billy Crystal, Tommy James, Norah Jones, Donny Hathaway, Curtis Mayfield . . .

On this particularly hot summer Monday night, I dropped by to hear the Oz Noy Trio.

Oz Noy is a virtuosic guitar player who blends jazz, funk, rock, blues, and R & B. The players in the trio change depending on their tour schedules, but Oz Noy is the mainstay. Many times it's Will Lee on bass. You've probably heard Lee play on David Letterman's Show in the Paul Shaffer Band. The drummers vary as well, but I've been fortunate to hear Keith Carlock and Dave Weckl play with Oz. Carlock plays with the band, Steely Dan, and Weckl has played with artists like Madonna, Paul Simon, and Chick Corea.

Upon entering the club, as I was paying the $15 cover charge, my wife, Susan, called my cell phone from Calgary.

I responded quickly with a text and found a seat near the front of the stage. I turned off my phone to await the performance.

It wasn't till the next morning when I looked at my text message to my wife.

"At the bitter end."

Bittersweet.

19. RIGHT AND LEFT

"That's not right!"

Amazingly enough, the comment can come from left-brain thinking. Imagine you're playing the piano and, in the middle of a creative passage, you stop and say it aloud. Your right brain is creatively in motion, and you stop when the comment from the left hemisphere of your brain halts the flow.

In a group rehearsal setting, one of the performers is playing through a long passage, and another stops the group and proclaims, "That's a wrong note!"

Now what? Correct the wrong note and get back to rehearsal? Ignore the comment? Does this affect the "groove" and "rhythm" of the rehearsal?

It can be very helpful to have both kinds of thinkers participating in the process of making music. With a strategy in place about how to rehearse, both kinds of thinkers can move the creative process forward effectively.

Focusing on a specific passage can be helpful. Break the passage into smaller chunks. Visualize where you want to go in the section, slow the speed of the passage.

A positive approach, a belief that you can do it, and a fearless attitude to overcome encourage a successful outcome.

Music actually affects every region of the brain. When all types of learners are engaged in rehearsal, the joy of music is at the heart of the process.

Do music for a lifetime. Over and over, you'll experience joy!

20. IMAGINE THAT

When working with singers, I try not to give too many directives, like "Stay grounded. Breathe low. Connect from the diaphragm. Open your throat. Place the sound higher in the mask."

That's too much information for the brain to decipher. The frontal lobe of the brain can only hold so much information—like a record or a CD. When we have too much information, we tend to forget. We're paralyzed from being in the moment. Long explanations are lost on the listener.

The brain works well with metaphors, images, and similes. Short, concise messages.

When relating to a particular vocal style or colour, it's helpful to offer a specific example to get results.

- To get immediate results from a singer, ask him or her to think about biting an apple when placing their vocal sound.

- Rather than *forcing* sound out as a singer, *take* the sound out as in the motion of removing an object from a bag.

- With an imaginary brush, paint an imaginary arch of blue onto an imaginary white canvas. That image will support a beautiful smooth flowing phrase for the singer.

- With both hands gripping a pillow, thrust it to the floor using both arms. Focus on the pillow lying on the floor. As a singer, visualize that's where the high notes live. Think high is low and low is high. It's exciting to hear the sound that a singer produces when he understands what the sound "feels like" in his head.

Identifying a strategy to achieve a goal is common practice; "how to execute" is at the heart of it. The "how" involves specific actions to prepare the singer for a great performance. Imagery, similes, metaphors, and analogies get immediate results.

Singing is like expressing your innermost feelings to your closest friend.

21. THE SENSES

What is the strongest of the five senses? If you were standing in pitch darkness about 40,000 years ago, what sense would provide the most detail to determine if there were a predator in your space? That's random . . . but play along.

Sight? It's quite immediate to register something at first sight, but in this instance, it's pitch dark. Sorry, Romeo.

Touch? It would be too late for you if a predator was within your grasp, even if the predator was the Killer Rabbit of Caerbannog in the film *Monty Python and the Holy Grail*.

Taste? It could be you who is tasted! Apparently, humans are pretty tasty to predators. Don't even think *Silence of the Lambs*.

Sound? It takes an eighth of a second to decode information about sound. That's quick. It really depends how far you are from the sound. Not the strongest of the senses in this moment. Predators don't care if you sing—they will still eat you anyway.

Smell? Yes, that's the most helpful one to determine whether there's a predator in your midst. Smell is connected to memory. Irene, an excellent jazz singer I coach, is a perfumer. She once worked with a psychology professor to "perfume" memories of clients. "There are one trillion different stimuli associated with smell. The sense of smell is directly connected to the hippocampus part of the brain," she explained. "So it doesn't need to go through short-term memory first like the other senses do. That means it has the deepest connection to our past."

Acting coach Konstantin Stanislavski spoke about use of the five senses when acting. It's helpful to utilize them when seeking the truth for your character inside the scene.

When using senses to tell a story, the brain plays an important role. There are sights, sounds, smells, touches, and tastes that the brain remembers and stories from our past that are quickly brought to our attention.

The best storytellers engage us through the senses—which is so effective when telling the story inside a song.

22. WRITING A SONG

There's a heady little song written by Harry Nilsson titled *"Good Old Desk"* (1968) that I often use as an example of good songwriting for new songwriters.

Harry Nilsson was gifted as a singer/songwriter and has produced a prolific discography of hundreds of songs. Some of his most popular songs performed and written include: *"One,"* a number-five hit on the Billboard Charts with Three Dog Night; *"Without You,"* the Badfinger song that Nilsson himself recorded which became a number one hit; *"Coconut,"* which charted number five in Canada; *"Me and My Arrow,"* written by Nilsson for an animated television movie featuring Ringo Starr as narrator; and his own release of Fred Neil's *"Everybody's Talkin'."* That song was the theme song to the Oscar-winning movie *Midnight Cowboy* and won a Grammy for Nilsson as Best Contemporary Vocal Performance Male. In 2015, Nilsson was voted number 62 in *Rolling Stone's* 100 Greatest Songwriters of All Time.

Jason Blume teaches a very successful Nashville Songwriters' Workshop on this very subject. When beginning the songwriting process, Blume notes how important it is to set a short time limit for writing, establishing that the writer should not be critical of anything that appears on his page during the early writing process and that anything created at this early stage is regarded as "excellent." Just get out of your way and write.

"Good Old Desk" is built on three verses: a simple chorus after each verse with an opening and closing tag. Each verse moves the song forward.

The first verse describes the desk, the second verse personifies the desk, and the third verse builds a relationship between the singer and his desk. As the song moves along, it becomes a little more elaborate musically. A few more instrumental sounds are added to complement the overall song colour.

Nilsson once shared with Hugh Hefner on the television show *Playboy After Dark* that *"Good Old Desk"* was about GOD—the acronym built from the song title. Years later, Nilsson said he was just joking.

"Good Old Desk" is a simple and smart song that offers creative insight into the art of writing a good song. Listen to the version of the song by Canadian singer-songwriter Ron Sexsmith—he does it right.

You'll know a good song the moment you experience it.

23. YOUR SIGNATURE SOUND

According to Canadian music producer Garth Richardson, the first eight seconds of a performance matter the most. Garth has engineered recordings for the Red Hot Chili Peppers; Nickelback and Mötley Crue. His father, Jack Richardson, is credited with producing the Guess Who, Alice Cooper, Badfinger, and Poco.

It's about your "sound" as an artist and your "look." What you see and hear is what you get. That's how your audience determines whether they want more. That's when Garth, the studio engineer, knows it's worth a serious listen.

Great performers prepare. In performance, it's about flow and being in the moment. Focus on the story—not on who's in the room, and not on the technical and challenging passages of your performance.

Malcolm Gladwell (2000) says, "Choking is about thinking too much. Panic is about thinking too little.

Choking is about loss of instinct. Panic is reversion to instinct" (p. 84).

To find your voice, avoid the crazy-making monkey chatter. Julie Cameron (1992), in her book *The Artist's Way*, describes crazy-makers. They're distractors and self-directed divas. Stay away from the crazy-makers and focus on *your* performance.

In time, you'll find your signature you. And so will your audience.

24. FOCUS FORWARD

This is a big one.

It stimulates creativity for the long term. It helps an artist to stay focused and positive. It's a way for an artist to stay centred on core values and beliefs. It keeps the *flow* of creativity alive.

To move forward, it's essential to stay positive. Throwing colleagues under the bus is never a good solution to resolving issues. Own it if it's yours to own, and let the long-term vision guide your resolution to do the right thing. Festering over unnecessary inside chatter draws you away from moving forward. Privately criticizing a colleague or another member of the team rarely results in a good outcome.

Go directly to that individual who is the cause of tension. At the same time, I've been advised by a close friend to "beware of people who invite you over for tea and hand grenades."

Listen. Talk with them and act based on values and principles inherent in the overall vision and mission of the organization. Then move on, move forward, turn the page, and focus forward.

It will clear your mind to make creative decisions down the road. It opens the window where creativity lives.

When you do the right thing, you will know.

PERFORM

Performing Forward

25. CLARITY OF PURPOSE

Distinguished psychologist and author, Daniel Kahneman (2011), defines the "Focusing Illusion" in *Thinking Fast and Slow*. "Nothing in life is as important as you think it is when you are thinking about it" (p. 402).

This is all well and good; however, we know that a long-term focus on vision, mission, and goals lead to a better outcome. We see this with the results of successful Olympic athletes.

Set a goal—set a purpose through a vision and mission, and results happen.

I spent three years with a group of colleagues building a vision/mission at Sir Winston Churchill High School in Calgary. It was part of my master's studies at San Diego State University and provided a long-term vision and mission for stakeholders at the school.

"In its complete sense, vision is a fervent belief in a unique, improved, attainable, future state for the organization. It is a 'passion for excellence' fuelled by deeply held values and unswerving commitment" (Braun, 1991, p. 12).

A mission statement is the written philosophy or creed of an organization. "It focuses on what you want to be (character), and to do (contributions and achievements), and on the values or principles upon which being and doing are based" (Covey, 1989, p. 113).

Clarity of purpose is the starting point along the journey. With the mission statement, there was an increased clarity of communication and commitment for what we wanted to be as teachers, as students, and as parents in this school. There was buy-in from all stakeholders. The school was presented with a special achievement award from the Government of Alberta at the end of the process.

Our document (1994) focused on six outcomes:

1. Partnering with parents

2. Pursuit of learning

3. Teaching by example

4. Preparation for the workplace

5. Social responsibility

6. Citizenship

The vision of the school is written into its current philosophy and values. For me, reading that document now, still provides a vision, a mission, and clarity of purpose for a better future.

Know where you're going and you'll get there . . . quicker.

26. THINKING ABOUT TOMORROW

Thinking about tomorrow can create new habits that help build new connections toward a successful future. Living in the moment is regarded as sacred by many. That's where *flow* is realized. However, when one is focused on the future, even greater possibilities can result. You see ahead.

It's like writing "morning pages" where one's self-conscience is released onto a blank page. Amazingly, some of these very thoughts become reality. Morning pages are explained by Julia Cameron (1992) in her breakthrough book, *The Artist's Way*. It's a stream of consciousness type of writing where anything and everything that crosses one's mind is written on the page. The whole process is a tool for creativity.

You can be proactive about your health. For example, if there is a slight indication that things aren't quite right, you notice that your walking gait is slowing, your steps are less assured, and your stride is slightly shorter. What would you do?

A specialist can relate that through deliberate exercise with a trainer or therapist, and with a positive approach, seniors can ward off the possibility of moving to an extended-care facility. They can live in their homes longer if they are proactive about their health.

Thinking about tomorrow can improve your today.

27. CREATING
NEW HABITS

Thinking ahead sometimes has to do with changing one's course of thinking to create new habits. You've heard the adage: same habits, same results.

When an individual is mentally locked in a specific paradigm while attempting to solve an issue, seeing the solution through new lenses can help. You might have the right answer to the wrong question. You might be caught in your own bias and not realize the other perspective or another possible option. You might be caught in autopilot and you feel there is no reason to change.

Even physically, when a person with Parkinson's disease suddenly freezes while walking, a change in direction can break the freeze. Moving to the right or to the left can start up motion again. It's like the low and slow sideways waddle of a penguin to free up the freeze.

Create new habits. Ask more questions. Keep the dialogue alive. Make a move. Shift your thinking.

28. BRAIN CHANGE

I had to say it a few times to get the rhythm of the word—
"basal ganglia."

The basal ganglia is the part of our brain that learns
a sequence of actions that are ultimately done without
thinking, like chewing gum, tying your shoes, or button-
ing your shirt.

Your energy to get things done is channeled through
the basal ganglia. Habits, rituals, and routines are formed
here. When we change a habit or set out to do something
new, it requires more effort. The cerebral cortex is respon-
sible for this higher order thinking.

Another term I pronounced a few times: "cerebral cortex."

The cerebral cortex is made up of four lobes: occipital
(vision); temporal (hearing, language, memory, object
and scene recognition); parietal (touch, temperature
processing, spatial processing, attention, visual guided
actions); and frontal (motor processing, memory, decision making).

The cortex helps us interact with the world around us. With a deliberate mindful and goal-directed focus, the cortex can override autopilot and move us toward creating effective new habits leading to new creative discoveries.

Constant innovation keeps our daily work fresh. Moving from old paradigms and past thinking requires a new approach. The cortex is the part of our brain that can help create these new habits.

To know is to know.

29. EPISTEMOLOGY

How do we know what we know?

A simplified definition of epistemology is "learning about learning."

For me, that's at the heart of growing and moving forward. I feel confident that as long as I continue to learn, there will be a good outcome.

After teaching for nineteen years in public schools, I decided to spend a full year talking with experts in education, pedagogy, and business. My wife was supportive; it was like a year's sabbatical of thinking and learning.

I met one on one with thinkers and held think tanks with groups at my studio in Calgary. We shared ideas about: how people learn, what is the purpose of school, what is necessary in education to prepare thinking for new technologies, and new approaches to problem solving.

It was a highly productive year that led me to what I currently do as a mentor and coach.

As we move into new global responsibilities, it's essential to realize that epistemology directs us to important discoveries about how we live and work together in the world.

Life's possibilities are endless, as we continue to learn.

30. POSSIBILITY

If you connect with people on the very simplest level of passion, they will do amazing things. It's about being fearless and addressing your fear by embracing what you love.

"Just do it." That brand, alongside the famous "swoosh," became a highly successful calling card for Nike. It resonated with millions of people. Nike has become the world's largest supplier and manufacturer of athletic shoes, apparel, and sports equipment.

Think about some of the most exciting and challenging times in your life when you stepped out fearlessly.

Maybe it was when you were a kid and you decided to play a new sport. Now you love that sport. You've become a fan. You travel to cities to watch your team play.

You were inspired by Eric Clapton's guitar playing, and your parents gifted you with your first guitar. Now you own a few guitars that you play regularly. And next month you're going to see Clapton live in concert.

You stood up to your fear of the bully. You were unafraid of the consequences. You knew it was important to overcome your fear. You *would* overcome. You made that decision.

Maybe you were afraid of not having enough. Money was tight. Yet you determined not to hold it tighter. You decided to invest in a future built on what you want to do and what you love to do.

Perhaps you love to gamble and you were down to your last few dollars. You borrowed money. Flew to Vegas. Got a hotel. Wait a minute! That's another story for another time . . .

It does matter who we surround ourselves with *and* why we spend time with certain individuals. People we meet inspire us to greater possibility thinking.

It's not about "lookin' good." It's about passion, purpose, and being fearless about stepping out.

Love what you do, and you'll love living the life you've chosen to live.

31. MINDFULNESS: A STORY

Summer Festival

Lilith Fair broke all the conventional paradigms for festival tours. Up to 1997, the *major* top-grossing summer tours included Pink Floyd, Michael Jackson, the Rolling Stones, David Bowie, Bruce Springsteen, U2, and the Eagles. These tours consisted of mostly male artists or male-led bands. At the time, concert promoters and radio stations refused to feature two female musicians in a row.

That changed after Lilith Fair. The festival was founded by Canadian singer/songwriter phenom Sarah McLachlan during the years 1997–99 and again in 2010. It showcased the "who's who" of female artists and female-led bands.

In 1997, Lilith Fair became the top-grossing tour festival of the summer. Over the first three years of the festival, Lilith performances sold out in some of the biggest amphitheatres, outdoor performance centres, pavilions, theatres, and fairgrounds in North America.

The Lilith Fair atmosphere was upbeat, motivating, supportive, highly creative, and engaging for the artists. Singers and band members travelled, ate, and played together. During the tour months (usually July and August), when Lilith performers had to attend to their own performances, other artists would take their place and join the Lilith tour. Artists invited other artists to perform onstage at Lilith, and the roster grew.

It was inspiring to share backstage stories with band members and artists like Sarah McLachlan, the Dixie Chicks, Fiona Apple, Bonnie Raitt, Chrissy Hynde, and Melanie Doane. My wife and I followed the career of Ashwin Sood, a former music student of ours who was drummer, background vocalist, and unofficial musical director with Sarah McLachlan's band. We were welcome to attend the Lilith tour at any tour stop. Ashwin and I continue to work together hosting workshops.

Significance

Lilith Fair was significant in so many ways. It followed the path of right-brainers who, according to Daniel H. Pink, will rule the future. These leaders shape and guide our world through six senses according to Pink (2005).

1. They create something that is engaging as in *design*.

2. They fashion a compelling narrative through the *story*.

3. They synthesize and put the pieces of the big picture together—like creating a *symphony*.

4. They forge relationships through *empathy*.

5. They know the importance of *play*.

6. They create *meaning* through purpose, transcendence, and spiritual fulfillment.

All this was at the heart of Lilith Fair in 1997–99. Artists were focused and prepared, anxiety and negativism were lost to a bigger and more positive narrative. Even as the televangelist and conservative activist Jerry Falwell dismissed Lilith Fair as a pagan event, Sarah McLachlan stood strong about its capacity to bring people together.

She was unafraid to fail, and no one on that tour was afraid of their ultimate successes.

Being fearless can lead to a greater self-awareness.

32. GRATITUDE

This might be the secret to it all!

Oprah Winfrey writes about it in her little book of treasures titled *What I Know For Sure*. Oliver Sacks writes about what it means to live a good and worthwhile life in one of his final books, *Gratitude*. The word appears on numerous book covers: *The Little Book of Gratitude*, *The Gratitude Diaries*, *The Psychology of Gratitude*, and so many more. Being grateful means taking the high road of life.

New York playwright, Adam Szymkowicz, expressed gratitude in this final monologue after a musical performance,

> Thank you! Thank you! Be my valentine. Eat cake with me. Start a cover band with me. Invent a new kind of soup. Thank you. Thank you. Thank you. Thank you. It's been everything.
> (Szymkowicz, 2018)

Expressing thankfulness brings joy like a gift passing from one happy presenter to a joyful receiver. Gratitude is the secret sauce inside a great relationship.

When was the last time you said, "Thank you"?

33. WHY I AM A TEACHER

On my way to my piano lesson as a kid, I would pick up a *Globe and Mail* at the corner newspaper box. Getting the paper was the request of my piano teacher. The price of the paper covered the cost of my piano lesson.

As I walked into his studio, I would hand him the paper. My teacher sat at a green easel-like artist's desk with a hookah pipe propped atop and a handful of easily accessible pencils. He laid the newspaper amongst his many desk props. A large dark brown upright Willis piano was positioned to his left. A few times his hookah pipe gurgled as I played a J. S. Bach *Intermezzo*.

The main room would be the living room in any other house, but this was his music room. Just off to the left of the entrance was another room—easels with canvases of artwork, some with finished oil paintings and others with charcoal sketches. This was his creative space.

He was the teacher who motivated me to ask questions, to make thoughtful musical decisions, to open my mind to all styles of music, and to musical performances. He was a Renaissance man: painter, church organist, television host, an authority on the Welland Ship Canal, an astrologer.

His name was Prynce Nesbitt. He possessed a brilliant mind and was a treasure for those who studied music with him. For me, he was my mentor.

He died when I was sixteen. At that time, I was offered anything from his trove of treasures. I chose his metronome, the timepiece that monitored rhythm and groove. I discovered so much more about Prynce Nesbitt the artist when I explored his writings and his artwork.

He was always fearless about doing the right thing— getting to the heart of music and sharing his gift with someone like me.

"Time has a wonderful way of showing us what really matters." —Margaret Peters

ABOUT THE AUTHOR

Brian Farrell is a respected vocal coach who lives in the Canadian foothills of the Rocky Mountains.

Brian is as unique as his projects and the artists he has collaborated with. His formal education includes a B.Mus. A. (Hons.) and B.Ed. from Western University in London, studies at Westminster Choir College in Princeton, Western Michigan University, and an M.A. from San Diego State University.

He has taught music for twenty-six years in schools and led choirs in churches for over thirty years. Working with Parkinson patients opened opportunities to learn more about the brain and music through collaborations with neurologists, neuroscientists, Parkinson patients, and their caregivers.

Brian Farrell Music Inc. was established to focus on vocal coaching, artistic mentorship, and music workshops including: Turntable Creative—a platform for singers to "try on their songs" for professional feedback; Reboot Lab—a workshop on the current landscape of the music business, and seasonal workshops to help singers develop their signature sound.

As a vocal coach, he has worked with hundreds of singers and speakers. In his twenty-four years as Artistic Director of Revv52, he collaborated with some of the finest talent to establish this unique Canadian performance ensemble that expands the bounds of artistic performance. The group has performed twice at Carnegie Hall in New York City, and hundreds of concerts in Alberta, Canada.

Brian lives in Calgary with his wife, Susan, who owns a financial education brokerage, and their dogs Gadsby and Duke. Their son Ryan is a urology surgeon in Chicago and their daughter Anna Lauren is a producer/director in NYC.

ACKNOWLEDGEMENTS

Thanks to Prynce Nesbitt, a great music mentor, and teacher—the one who set this all into motion. And to the teachers along the way who inspired excellence—Dr. Marino at San Diego State University was one of them.

To my wife, Susan, who looks at life with a glass more than half full and to our kids who already make a difference in the lives of many. They help people.

And to those who step out in the world fearless to do the right thing—even when the rhythm of time ticks against their internal clock.

REFERENCE LIST

Arden, P. (2006). *Whatever you think, think the opposite.* New York, NY: Penguin Books, Ltd.

Blume, J. (2003). *Inside songwriting: Getting to the heart of creativity.* New York, NY: Watson-Guptill Publications.

Braun, J. (1991). *An analysis of principal leadership vision and its relationship to school climate.* (Unpublished doctoral dissertation). Northern Arizona University, Flagstaff.

Brizendine, L. (2006). *The female brain.* New York, NY: Broadway Books.

Brown, J. & Fenske, M. (2010). *The winner's brain.* Cambridge, MA: Da Capo Press.

Byrne, D. (2012). *How music works.* San Francisco, CA: McSweeney's.

Cameron, J. (1992). *The artist's way.* New York, NY: Penguin Putnum, Inc.

Colvin, G. (2010). *Talent is overrated: What really separates world-class performers from everybody else.* New York, NY: Penguin Books, Ltd.

Covey, S. R. (1989). *The seven habits of highly effective people.* New York, NY: Simon and Schuster.

Coyle, D. (2012). *The little book of talent: 52 tips for improving your skills.* New York, NY: Bantam Books.

Csikszentmihalyi, M. (1990). *Flow: The psychology of optimal experience.* New York, NY: HarperCollins Publishers.

Csikszentmihalyi, M. (1996). *Creativity: Flow and the psychology of discovery and invention.* New York, NY: HarperCollins Publishers.

Farrell, B. (1994). *Building a vision and mission at Sir Winston Churchill high school.* (Unpublished master's thesis). San Diego State University, CA.

Farrell, B. (2007–2016). *Blog posts.* Retrieved from www. brianfarrell.ca

Gladwell, M. (2000, August 21). The art of failure. *The New Yorker*, p. 84.

Goleman, D. (1995). *Emotional Intelligence.* New York, NY: Bantam Books.

Grimes, William. (1996, December 2). Tiny Tim: Singer, dies at 64; flirted, chastely, with fame. *New York Times.* Retrieved from https://www.nytimes.com/1996/12/02/

arts/tiny-tim-singer-dies-at-64-flirted-chastely-with-fame.
html

Horstman, J. (2010). *The scientific American brave new brain*. San Francisco, CA: John Wiley and Sons, Inc.

Jensen, E. (1998). *Teaching with the brain in mind*. Alexandria, VA: ASCD Publications.

Jensen, E. (2000). *Music with the brain in mind*. San Diego, CA: The Brain Store, Inc.

Kahneman, D. (2011). *Thinking fast and slow*. Toronto, ON: Doubleday Canada.

Kaufman, Michael T. (1994, October 14). The hotel in Chelsea that art calls home. *New York Times*. Retrieved from https://www.nytimes.com/1994/10/14/arts/the-hotel-in-chelsea-that-art-calls-home.html

Laing, R.D. (1972). *Knots*. New York, NY: Vintage Books.

Langer, E. J. (2014). *Mindfulness*. Boston, MA: Da Capo Press.

Leonard, G. (1992). *Mastery: The keys to success and long-term fulfillment*. New York, NY: Penguin Books, Ltd.

Levetin, D. J. (2006). *This is your brain on music: The science of human obsession*. Toronto, ON: Penguin Group, Canada.

Levitin, D. J. (2008). *The world in six songs*. Toronto, ON: Penguin Group, Canada.

Margulis, E. H. (2014). *On repeat: How music plays the mind*. New York, NY: Oxford University Press.

May, R. (1975). *The courage to create*. New York, NY: W. W. Norton & Company.

Palfreman, J. (2015). *Brain storms: The race to unlock the mysteries of Parkinson's disease*. New York, NY: Farrar, Straus and Giroux.

Penick, H. (1992). *Harvey Penick's little red book: Lessons and teachings from a lifetime in golf*. New York, NY: Simon and Schuster.

Pink, D. H. (2005). *A whole new mind: Why right-brainers will rule the future*. New York, NY: Penguin Books, Ltd.

Sacks, O. (2007). *Musicophilia*. New York: NY: Alfred A. Knopf, Inc.

Sprenger, M. (1999). *Learning and memory: The brain in action*. Alexandria, VA: ASCD Publications.

Stanislavski, K. (1936). *Building a character* (3rd ed.). New York, NY: Routledge.

Stephens-Davidowitz, S. (2018, February 10). Sunday Review. *New York Times*.

Sylwester, R. (1995). *A Celebration of neurons: An educator's guide to the human brain*. Alexandria, VA: ASCD Publications.

Szymkowicz, A. (2018). Earcandy: Can't get it out of my head. Unpublished manuscript.

Williams, B., Gluck, D. & Thompson, B. (2011). *Rhythms of the game: The link between music and athletic performance*. Milwaukee, WI: Hal Leonard Publishing Co.

Winfrey, O. (2014). *What I know for sure*. New York, NY: Flatiron Books.

Wolfe, P. (2001). *Brain matters: Translating research into classroom practice*. Alexandria, VA: ASCD Publications.

Wooten, V. (2006). *The music lesson: A spiritual search for growth through music*. New York, NY: Berkley Publishing Group.

Zander, R. S. & Zander, B. (2000). *The art of possibility*. New York, NY: Penguin Books, Ltd.